NINJA

Vol. 5
Lore of the
Shinobi Warrior

Text and verses
by Stephen K. Hayes

Edited by Mike Lee

Graphic Design by Sergio Onaga

Photography by Doug Churchill

Additional Photos by Stephen K. Hayes

Front Cover Art and Drawings by Gregory Manchess

Back Cover Photography by Rick Hustead

©1989 Ohara Publications, Inc.

All Rights Reserved

Printed in the United States of America

Library of Congress Control Number: 80-84678

ISBN-10: 0-89750-123-3

ISBN-13: 978-0-89750-123-1

Twelfth Printing 2007

WARNING

BLACK BELT BOOKS

A Division of **OHARA** 🔟 **PUBLICATIONS, INC.**

World Leader in Martial Arts Publications

Dedication
This volume is dedicated to the memory of Tom Bennich, happy warrior
who so encouraged me in my first years on the martial path.

ABOUT THE AUTHOR

International adventurer Stephen K. Hayes spent over 20 years in the pursuit of perfection through the study of the Oriental martial arts and meditation techniques handed down by the esoteric Diamond Thunderbolt tradition. In his travels throughout the world, he has studied with teachers ranging from the grandmaster of Japan's ninja shadow warriors to the Dalai Lama of Tibet.

In the autumn of 1985, Hayes was awarded a place in the BLACK BELT Hall of Fame for his years of pioneering work in introducing the ninja "art of accomplishment through invisible action" to the American public. As international director of the Shadows of Iga Society, Hayes continues to travel the world to train for his own advancement with Japanese and Tibetan teachers, bridging East and West with the timeless knowledge of self-transformation and personal power cultivation once reserved for only a special few of the world's population.

As the first American ever to be accepted as a direct disciple of ninjutsu grandmaster Masaaki Hatsumi of Noda City, Japan, Stephen K. Hayes was exposed to an art that was, until the early 1970s, totally unknown to all but a handful of practitioners who had managed to gain entrance to the grandmaster's dojo. In September of 1978, Stephen K. Hayes became the first non-Japanese person in the history of the art of ninjutsu ever to be awarded the title of *Shidoshi*, (teacher of the warrior ways of enlightenment).

Today, Hayes travels throughout North America, Europe, and Asia as a teacher, seminar leader, and lecturer. His informative and inspiring presentations translate his extensive background in the Oriental combat and meditation arts into practical lessons for handling the pressures, choices, uncertainties, and stresses of life in the modern Western world. Hayes' interpretation of Japan's warrior path of enlightenment creates a basis for understanding the power of directed intention as a tool for accomplishment in all areas of living.

CHAPTER ONE
Lessons Behind the Lessons: A personal reflection of progress in the art of the shadow warrior—Stephen K. Hayes recalls how his early years of teaching the true art of ninjutsu became a period of even higher learning 7

CHAPTER TWO
Myths of Ninjutsu: Sorting fact from fiction—A detailed explanation of the truth behind the popular misconceptions about ninjutsu 17

CHAPTER THREE
Ninpo Taijutsu: Movement as art—Fundamental techniques of ninja body movement in combat, including body attitudes, three ranges of reach, three angles of impact, three height levels, three methods of delivery dynamics, and striking tools 27

CHAPTER FOUR
Jissen No Ho: Self-defense fighting—Eleven examples of using ninja fighting techniques and additional ground control methods in self-defense 105

AFTERWORD
An Interview with Stephen K. Hayes—The author answers questions asked by attendees of special seminars conducted at his personal training hall 149

CHAPTER ONE

In the words and actions
  of the wise
  there can arise
  the appearance of contradiction.

Know confidently that the accumulation of
  experience
  tempered by
  awareness
  will eventually banish any of the confusion
  that plays servant to
  smallness of vision.

LESSONS BEHIND THE LESSONS

A personal reflection of progress
in the art of the shadow warrior

Remember to avoid the temptation of seeing yourself as a teacher,"
admonished Dr. Masaaki Hatsumi, 34th grandmaster of the
Togakure Ryu ninjutsu tradition and *soke* of eight other warrior
ryu as well.

My mentor and I were drinking Japanese green tea together on a rainy
Sunday evening in August of 1980. We sat on *tatami* (straw mats) at a low
table in the grandmaster's home. The doctor's extensive collection of carved
classical Japanese masks stared down from all four walls of the room as
though to eavesdrop on our conversation. Having completed the first major
portion of my apprenticeship under the personal direction of Dr. Hatsumi, I
was to leave the ninja school in Noda City, Japan, and go out into the world
on my own. Certainly I would be permitted to come back to Japan to visit my
teacher whenever I wanted, but the point that Dr. Hatsumi seemed to be making was the fact that I needed time on my own, away from the comfort and

security of being a student in the home of the grandmaster of ninjutsu. By being cut off from my teacher for awhile, I would have the opportunity to experience challenges and pressures in the unpredictable world outside the safety of the dojo.

As always, the grandmaster's lesson seemed perplexingly contradictory to me. In September of 1978, I had become the first non-Japanese person in the history of the art of ninjutsu ever to earn the title of *shidoshi*, (teacher of the warrior ways of enlightenment). My *menjo* (diploma) was a license permitting me to establish my own independent training hall, and had been handwritten by the grandmaster himself. The huge document bore the *hanko* seals of authority that had been used by the family for generations. Now I was being sent away from the school with the title of teacher, along with the admonition to avoid seeing myself as a teacher.

In my years as Masaaki Hatsumi's personal student, I had learned not to question paradox. Indeed, the appearance of contradiction often seemed to be an integral part of most lessons. I knew the man well enough to know that finding the answer to that question was part of my assignment out in the world beyond Japan. I would figure it out later.

"Be wary whenever you reach the point where you feel that you have finally gotten down to the bottom line as to the essence of the warrior arts," the grandmaster continued. "To reach the bottom line is the same thing as being dead."

This would be our last night together as master and student before I left to take up the warrior path alone for the next several years. I already felt twinges of nostalgia for the future's past that was yet the present moment. I knew that this night and its significance would be looked back upon as a milestone in my life. I acknowledged the fact that from this night forward I would never be able to return to the comfort of knowing that as an apprentice, my teacher was always right around the corner in case I ran into difficulty. It was a frightening and yet at the same time exciting moment.

I was hoping to gain some last-minute perspectives on how to find that bottom line while out in the world so far away from my teacher and seniors at the dojo. Being warned that finding the bottom line was akin to death was the last thing that I wanted to hear at that point. Though the testing journey had yet to actually begin, I suddenly felt myself grow very weary.

I so wanted to do a good job of representing my teacher's art in the United States. This would be the first exposure that Western world martial artists would have to the legendary art of Japan's ninja invisible warriors. My unique position as the only American ever to be trained in the art of ninjutsu was at the same time a great honor and a great burden. It would be up to me, and me alone, to establish the identity of Masaaki Hatsumi's ninja warrior legacy in North America. The job I did would perhaps determine whether or not I would be permitted to return some day in the future to once again take up my role as an *uchi-deshi* (home student) of the grandmaster in order to further explore higher levels of warrior power under his guidance.

"Ultimately, you must not allow yourself to be consumed by striving for strength as opposed to weakness, hardness as opposed to softness, or speed as opposed to slowness in the warrior arts. The only way to attain total invincibility is to let go of concern with the limitations of the body, and allow yourself to become one with the *ku no seikai* (void realm) that will permit you complete freedom of adapting." The grandmaster brushed the Japanese characters in black ink on a sheet of rice paper, and informed me to display the admonition in any dojo that I was to establish in my home country.

Again I was confronted by internal conflict and confusion. In America, where speed and power were considered the only standard criteria for determining martial prowess, how was I to prove my art? There were no kata that I could perform, my methods would not fit the limitations of the contest ring, and the subtle sensitivity to the energy of the fight would be impossible to portray graphically on the movie screen. Short of actual damaging combat with an attacking aggressor, it was going to be very difficult making an impression on the martial artists of my native country without spectacular displays of the speed and power that the grandmaster considered a hindrance to warrior development.

As I walked along the rain-slicked side streets of Noda City that night in 1980, I knew that I was on the threshold of a great adventure. Returning to my native land to offer a martial art that no one else there had ever experienced would be a fascinating test of my own ability to make things happen. How would this art be received in the land of group kata to rock music, American flag karate suits with red rubber boxing gloves, and the post-Bruce Lee era modernist disdain for relying on the combat training methods that had been handed down by Oriental warrior masters for generations? What if no one else in the States was interested in my combat and enlightenment art at all? What if the sports arts really were the wave of the future in the West, and I was to be received as some sort of bizarre anachronism with my insistence on combat application realism and personal responsibility for the prevention of danger? The prospect of my future was at the same time exciting and terrifying.

As it turned out, I arrived in the United States just in time to witness the birth of what would later be referred to as the "ninja boom" of the 1980s. As the months quickly flew by, the art of ninjutsu was propelled forward to

become the most talked about and controversial force to hit the martial arts community since the emergence of the Bruce Lee phenomenon. Many movie makers, book and magazine publishers, mail-order merchants, and television producers all grabbed up the fascinating allure of the ninja to promote their projects and run up their profits.

With all the publicity generated by my story as the first American ever taught the art of ninjutsu in Japan by the grandmaster, I was no longer concerned with how to go about getting people to notice my art. That stage seemed well behind me. I had to be concerned with how to prevent the commercial forces from completely taking over my art and transforming it into a monster that even the grandmaster could no longer recognize.

I began to concentrate on the task of educating the martial arts community as to just what the true art of the ninja was, commercialism and sensationalism aside. Through books and magazine articles, I worked to inform the public that ninjutsu was *not* solely an art of assassination and employment of dark powers, as seemed to be the prevaling stereotype, but was instead an approach to the prevention of danger based on harmony with the natural environment, scientific analysis of intelligence, and an intuitive attunement with the energy of events coming into manifestation around us. The true historical ninja operated out of love and responsibility for his family, and not for mere money or the thrill of murderous violence as is so often intimated in less knowledgeable authors' books on the subject.

Rather than attempt to settle in one place with training hall responsibilities that would restrict my mobility and my freedom to explore and learn, I first established the Shadows of Iga Festival as an annual event in Ohio and then set out on a tour of seminars all around the North American continent. Newly found friends who came to adopt the *ninpo* life-style as their own went on to organize groups of enthusiasts in their home areas, and I began to build up a small network of students despite my refusal to sit down and concentrate on creating a tightly controlled organization.

My own personal goal was still the same one that had taken me across the Pacific to Japan on that daring gamble in the first place those many years ago. I wanted knowledge and skill, all the knowledge and skill that was possible to gain, that would lead me to eventual mastery of the warrior arts of combat and enlightenment. I traveled throughout North America, Europe, the Himalayas, and the Orient looking for martial artists, military and espionage professionals, and combat veterans with whom I could compare my art and skills. Sometimes the knowledge comparisons took the form of demonstrations and reflections on other's past experience stories. Sometimes the comparisons took the more pointed form of actual bloody confrontations in which I was required to deal with hostile individuals who wanted to put my claims to the test.

Slowly and subtly, without even realizing it at first, I began to come to an understanding of my teacher's parting admonitions. In confrontations and skill tests against younger, faster, and stronger opponents, I was forced to muster up some quality beyond speed and strength and even technique itself in order to come out on top. I began to become more and more aware of experiencing what I would have to describe as something along the lines of supraphysical energy fields and forces that extended beyond mere strategy and technique application. On some occasions, it was as though I could tell where the attacker was headed before he even set into motion. As an experiment, I began to purposely decrease my own speed, and then worked at easing up on the bone and muscle tension behind my techniques. I was shocked to find that I actually had an easier time fitting in with my attacker's dynamics, and could more deftly use the momentum of my body, rather than the motion of my limbs alone, to down training partners who flew at me full speed.

It was something about the dynamics of the clash being experienced as a single unit of energy, as opposed to the separate energies of two independent contenders, that seemed to allow me to feel the attackers' intentions.

It became a somewhat humorously embarrassing regular occurrence at seminars. A spontaneous technique would just happen, based on the unexpected sudden motions of an attacker. When the students would inevitably request to see the technique again, I was often unable to recreate the identical movements a second time. I would attempt to explain that the energy directing the flow was different the second time, the attacker moved with slightly different dynamics or altered momentum and tension, so that the initial technique was not appropriate the second time and would not "let itself happen" naturally. Because of the difference in energy details the second time around, I had to do something different in order to down the attacker. For many martial artists trained to believe in systems of rigid form classification and cataloging of techniques, my own retreat into realms of unexplainable formless "energies" must have been the height of frustration.

Though I could perceive my own skills improving as I gathered experience away from my teacher, I was curious as to the reason for my growing inability to verbally express and teach those skills to others in a scientific manner. I slowly began to wonder if my inability to teach might perhaps be the first step toward experiencing the beginning stages of familiarity with the "void realm" that my teacher had emphasized as lying beyond the mechanics of speed and power and technique.

The more I continued to explore the interlocking disciplines of technique, energy sensitivity, mental flexibility, and channeled intention, whether in exercises involving unarmed combat, weapon work, stalking and evasion scenarios, or even non-martial, real-life challenges, the more I began to understand the grandmaster's words of warning concerning "getting to the bottom line" as to the essence of the warrior arts. The more carefully and scientifically one can describe and explain the process of prevailing in a murderous attack situation, the more subtle yet crucial elements one is forced to leave out for the sake of a clear description. Therefore, the more clear one is as to what the truth is, the more likely it is that he is farther away from the whole truth in its ultimate form.

It is a great lesson in the warrior arts to realize that the more tenaciously one clings to the comfort of any given theory, the more firmly prevented he is from exploring other possibilities and therefore growing in his knowledge. As grandmaster Hatsumi had warned, getting down to that bottom line conviction that we know all there is to know is the same thing as being dead. In the sense that to experience no more growth is akin to being dead, the warning is valid. In the grimmer realities of the martial arts, the man who has willfully stopped his growth by proclaiming himself a master faces the all too real prospect of defeat at the hands of a warrior who has discovered the power that is available to one who will never settle for yesterday's lessons. By dwelling in the realms of unclarity, one is forced to seek ever onward for the elusive truth that always waits one step beyond the next lesson that life brings.

As I continued my own personal quest for exploration of growth in personal power through the warrior tradition of ninjutsu, a distinct and decidedly distasteful public image of the art seemed to grow up around me. Curiously, this public image, fostered by many movies, television, novels, and increasing numbers of ninjutsu textbooks and magazine articles written by persons with no experience in the authentic art whatsoever, began to deviate more and more from the actual history and purpose of the art I had brought back with me on my return from Japan. I increased my efforts to turn the image back toward one more in keeping with the authentic history behind the art.

Ironically, directing my attention toward salvaging the reputation of the art that was so dear to me brought me face to face with an understanding of Dr. Hatsumi's initial admonition. As I reluctantly evolved into the position of spokesman for the art of ninjutsu, I began to encounter growing resistance to my message. While many martial artists claimed to have found great inspiration in the art I was introducing, others felt threatened and moved to confront my progress through the media.

The fact was predictable that I would not be America's "only ninja" for long. Within one year of my return to the United States and the subsequent

publicity it generated, there began to appear growing numbers of martial arts teachers suddenly attempting to convince the public that they too were masters of the ninja arts. The allure of the ninja image was just too strong for these people to resist, it seems. The world was soon subjected to all the highly dubious claims of those who clamored to jump upon the ninja bandwagon in the wake of the publicity given to my work in the Togakure Ryu.

This sudden emergence of those persons hoping to capitalize on the excitement and publicity surrounding this newly introduced art is not necessarily bad; it did, however, cloud up the issue as to just what true ninjutsu is. Many of these self-styled ninjutsu authorities wrote their own books and articles emphasizing savage and brutal training, flaunting hidden murder weapons, and reflecting the antisocial viewpoints characteristic of those persons who have allowed themselves to degenerate into neurotic realms of self-pity and feelings of victimization at the hands of society. Soon, newspapers began to carry accounts of criminals and lunatics carrying out robberies and murders while clad in mail-order ninja suits. Unlicensed ninja schools began popping up in all cities across the country, luring the young and impressionable into their morbid influence.

Hundreds of letters per week poured into my office from people around the world who wanted to know the truth behind all the stories and claims that they had read. Gradually, as the months turned into years, I began to realize that policing the image of the treasured art my teacher had given me was growing into a task that was beyond my limits. Interestingly enough, there was also a certain segment of the world that seemed to want the art to be all those twisted or morbid things it was not. I slowly came to realize that ultimately it could not be my responsibility to educate all persons as to what the true art of ninjutsu encompasses. The beauty and power of the ninja tradition had been misunderstood for centuries by all but those who personally lived the art, so where was the urgent need now to change the course of history?

Perhaps I had finally broken through to begin to learn what Masaaki Hatsumi had meant that night those years ago when he admonished me to avoid the temptation of considering myself a teacher. Being the one to educate all the others is an unending job. Ultimately, the art of the *shinobi* (invisible) warrior tradition is an extremely personal and demanding one, not meant to be easy to understand or convenient to package for the mass market consumer. The student enters a path with no end and sets out on a journey of discovery. The subtle irony is that the one who would prematurely label himself a teacher must by necessity *cease his journey* and begin to look backward for the sake of others who would be warriors. Thus ends the development of his own martial skills.

My own path of discovery now looks somewhat different than I had once imagined the future to be. Over the years, thousands of others have joined me on this adventure that is the lore of the shinobi warrior, and now those students are carrying the message of joy in movement and power of directed intention to other new participants around the world. Happily, there is no longer any need for a Stephen Hayes to single-handedly champion the ninja's combat art of enlightenment, now that there are so many authentic practitioners who have taken up the challenge of making this warrior enlightenment system operate in the world. I have after my years of work been freed to resume the path of the warrior quest, once more rededicated to the discovery of expanded knowledge in all forms.

That was, after all, the lesson my teacher seemed to challenge me to uncover when he sent me out into the world on my own all those years ago. How interesting it is that the ultimate secrets are always right there in front of us, if only we have collected enough experience and cultivated enough insight to see them.

CHAPTER TWO

Kyojitsu ten kan
Truth in the guise of falsehood
falsehood disguised as truth.

The ninja's powers of illusion
rely on the mind's insistence that
what we wish to see
indeed takes the form of
that which we seem to see.

MYTHS OF NINJUTSU
Sorting fact from fiction

Since the practice of the authentic Japanese art of ninjutsu was introduced to the Western world in the late 1970s, many false notions and erroneous impressions have grown up around the legendary shadow warriors known as the ninja. Many of these misconceptions have roots in fact, but have developed as falsehoods over the centuries of secrecy that have surrounded the art. Many of the incorrect ideas have grown out of a lack of discrimination between truth and falsehood on the part of moviemakers and book publishers. Also, some of the negative myths are the direct work of those outside the tradition who felt they had reason to fear the authentic ninja legacy.

The following popular myths embody several of the most common falacies and misconceptions. Following each inaccurate statement is a clarification of fact that better describes the truth behind the legends.

• *Ninjutsu is the dark side of the martial arts, the clandestine techniques of stealth, intelligence gathering, and assassination.*

The art of ninjutsu was born of a unique set of cultural, political, religious, and economic forces that played themselves out a thousand years ago in Japanese history. History's authentic ninja were a counterculture society forced into existence by the shifting fortunes of feudal Japanese political and military conflicts.

Contrary to common misconception, the ninja were not unsophisticated and superstitious low-class peasants. The ninja were the descendents of powerful noble warriors who, through the inevitable workings of fate, happened to be allied in support of powerful warlords who ultimately did not succeed in the collection of battles that made up the war for supremacy. With the defeat of their side's cause, these noble warriors were forced into lives of exile, dwelling in the mountain stretches of wilderness to the south of the Heian-kyo (now Kyoto) capital. These original ancestors of the ninja were then barred forever from the professions of state administration, trade, military command, and public service to which at one time they had successfully devoted their energies.

As exiles concerned with the rugged demands of survival in a harsh natural environment and a deadly political climate, the ninja families of south central Japan were forced to alter their tactics and strategies to better suit their precarious status. In truth, no one wanted to be a ninja; such status was a burden inflicted by fate. The ninja were the "underdogs," the oppressed hounded by a well-financed and mechanically ruthless government intent on stamping out any and all possible threats to its supremacy and control. Thus, subtle and shadowed means grew to take the place of the bold and forceful ways utilized by those persons holding power. Since the ninja families' numbers were so much smaller than those of the ruling powers that worked to eradicate them, intelligence gathering became a vastly more important task than troop drilling. With the very survival of the family at stake, the ninja warriors of Iga were required to devise a whole new approach to warfare, and the motivation behind that approach has been misunderstood for centuries.

- *The historical ninja of feudal Japan would serve any master who offered the right amount of cash.*

Because the historical ninja of five centuries ago in Japan served his own family and community above all else, he was highly unlikely to swear allegiance to any one military ruler. The military ally who found it convenient to link forces with the ninja family one day could just as easily change his needs and priorities the next day and turn his forces against his former ally. Such was the conduct of military aggression and government greed that characterized the *Sengoku Jidai* (Warring States Period) of Japanese history. Therefore, the ninja was only as loyal as suited his family's needs.

The ninja fought to retain his rights to dwell unhindered in the mountains that enshrined the ashes of his father's grandfather. His cultural and political opposite, the samurai, more often fought for other reasons. Territorial governorships and the right to appropriate heavy taxes from the local inhabitants were often the political rewards for siding with a military dictator who eventually conquered all rivals. Therefore, the samurai often found himself maintaining order in a region far from his ancestral home.

Unhindered by rigid codes of honor that could force other more conventional men into suicidal actions despite their own better judgment, the historical ninja was free to employ his common sense in order to accomplish needed objectives while reducing personal vulnerability. Naturally, from the culturally biased viewpoint of the samurai historians of the time, the ninja who would not play along and pledge undying loyalties to one political dictator was seen as the lowest form of mercenary.

- *The black suit, hood, and mask symbolize the essence and character of the art of ninjutsu.*

In truth, the historical ninja of feudal Japan probably never wore anything that looked at all like what we would call a "ninja suit" today. Ironically enough, the infamous ninja costume *(shinobi shozoku),* that has now made so much money for martial arts toy manufacturers, was most likely a product of the popular entertainment media of the 18th century in Japan. The *Kabuki* theater of the time relied on crews of black-clad scene changers and prop handlers. They were ignored as "invisible" by theatergoers who through necessity played along with the game in order to enjoy the dramatic illusions on stage (just as we in the Western world have learned to ignore as "invisible" the strings that control marionette puppet actions). Eventually, as the Kabuki plays began to include ninja characters in the story lines, some creative individual came up with the idea to use the "invisible" prop handlers' black costume as a visual trick to suggest the invisibility of the ninja character to the audience. Up until that time, the ninja in plays and art were usually depicted as being clothed in conventional warrior dress of the period.

In the historical ninjutsu reference work *Shoninki,* written by Natori Sanjuro Fuji Iisui, the traditional ninja operational costume colors are listed as subdued greens and browns, dark persimmons (black or gray-toned oranges), rusts, navy blues, and black. These colors were commonly worn by the people of the times, and therefore were excellent choices for the ninja's concealment costumes. In darkness of night, pure black tends to stand out too much, actually being darker than shadows and thereby creating the effect of a black shape in the darkness. Dull orange, maroon, or gray are colors that blend into the shadows much more effectively.

It is also highly likely that the historical ninja of feudal Japan rarely, if ever, wore black masks and hoods as is so often indicated in the popular entertainment literature of both Japan and the Western world. This costume affectation is also probably a cultural innovation spurred by the Kabuki plays of the peaceful ages under the rule of the Tokugawa family dictators.

There is nonetheless a proper method for tying on a breath-muffling mask, should such a tool be needed. Interestingly enough (or perhaps predictably enough), such a mask would be a far cry from the comical commercial toys being hustled to the public through ads in martial arts magazines. In the backward commercial products, the head and face components are always reversed and worn inside-out. The mask covers the face and then a cowl-like piece is tied on around the head. You have seen this silly backward set-up in all the sensationalist ninja movies made in the USA. This arrangement will not work, of course, as the cowl will easily shift around in the wind, all that cloth will block sound from the ears, and the overhanging lip of fabric that frames the face will make an excellent handle for an adversary to grab when he needs to control the ninja.

Today, some practitioners of the ninja arts will occasionally appear in the stereotypical dress because it is somehow expected of them. The illustrations in this series of books written by this author often feature such antique suits as a way of stimulating the imaginations of the readers. More often, however, authentic practitioners of ninjutsu today wear a simple black karate style *doji* (training suit) with the trouser legs tucked into the tops of a pair of split-toed *tabi* (footwear). For outdoor work in the woods or field, authentic practitioners have adapted Western-style black military or hunting garments for their training wear. Utilizing the garb of the current time and culture is much more in keeping with the true spirit of the shinobi arts than is clinging to a museum stereotype.

• *The historical ninja wore a chain mail shirt beneath his operational jacket, because the mail was more flexible than the traditional samurai plate armor.*

The common Japanese ninja comic book image always portrays the night warrior with cross-hatched lines at his wrists and throat, suggesting chain link armor under the cloth top of the operational costume. In truth, the extremely heavy weight of the iron or steel links made the wearing of *kusarikatabira* (chain mail armor) extremely rare. For espionage or sabotage guerrilla tactics, where lightness and speed were needed, the weight of the armor was too high a price to pay for the remote possibilities that the protection provided by the armor would be needed. The ninja's chain mail armor was more likely adopted only on the rare occasions when the extreme weight of the armor was justifiable in terms of required protection dictated by close-combat danger on a battlefield or in a war zone.

* *With a quick toss of a smoke or concussion grenade, an ambushed ninja could create an opening for his escape.*

Historically, the ninja's flares, firearms, smoke bombs, rocket arrows, and stun grenades all incorporated a black power explosive base. Niter, sulfur, and willow wood charcoal were mixed in specific proportions with alcohol usually derived from *sake* (rice wine), kneaded together, and dried. As such, this historical black power was incapable of being ignited through mere friction or shock, as is so often depicted in ninja movies. In reality, the black powder mixture required a burning fuse for ignition, therefore also requiring some sort of mechanism for setting the fuse on fire in the first place. The state of the art of feudal Japanese pyrotechnics rules out the possibility of so many scenes that we are used to seeing in which escaping ninja agent tosses out an unseen packet which suddenly detonates to the surprise of following enemies.

* *The traditional ninja wore his sword tied diagonally across his back, whereas the samurai carried his sword tucked in his sash at his side.*

The ninja with his sword tied to his back is a popular image, but one highly inaccurate in the light of history. When protruding up from behind, the sword would become a deadly hindrance to effective concealment, escape through tight spaces, or climbs through rafters and tree limbs. Rolling on the ground as a part of concealed escapes and hand-to-hand combat tactics would also be ruled out by the stereotypical ninja sword across the back.

Typically, the ninja used his sword as a cutting tool, club, scouting probe in the darkness, climbing aid, and as a carrier for blinding material. Therefore, the ninja most often carried his short sword in hand or tucked into his sash at his left side. From its position in the ninja's sash, the sword could be slipped around to the back or the front, or simply pulled out, to prevent it from becoming an obstacle. Indeed, certain ninja sword combat techniques employ a body configuration with the drawn blade in the right hand and the empty scabbard in the left.

The ninja's *shinobigatana* (sword) did incorporate a very long *sageo* (scabbard cord), however, which could be used to tie the sword across the back for occasions like long-distance running or underwater progression. When carried across the back, the ninja sword was most often worn with the hilt above the shoulder blade to facilitate easier drawing if needed.

- *The ninja's sword is short, straight-bladed, and features a large square* **tsuba** *(hand guard).*

Another cultural stereotype, the image of the short and straight ninja sword with its huge square tsuba probably came from two likely sources. From one viewpoint, it might be argued that since the ninja were legally barred from owning swords, the swords that they did come up with were probably homemade slabs of iron or steel that were ground to a cutting edge on a fairly crude stone sharpener. Straight blades were probably easier to forge than the gently curving works of art turned out by the master swordmakers commissioned by the powerful and moneyed samurai families. For the same reasons, a homemade utilitarian sword guard would most likely be little more than a flat, unadored square of steel.

As a second possible source of origin, it could be mentioned that the *choku-to* (straight-bladed short sword) could have been a stereotypical depiction of the straight sword brandished by images of the wrathful Buddhist deity Fudo Myo-oh, often cited as a patron guardian of the ninja families who protected the *mikkyo* (esoteric Buddhist) temples southeast of the ancient capitals of Kyoto and Nara. The oversized tsuba could also be another exaggeration adopted from the Kabuki stage.

In truth, a gracefully curving blade is a much better cutting instrument in a fight than is a straight blade. It is interesting to note that the majority of the better ninja swords in the personal collection of grandmaster Masaaki Hatsumi have curved blades, small oval tsuba hand guards, and scabbards several inches longer than the blades.

- *Today's elite military small unit tactics are the modern Western version of* **ninjutsu.**

Though it has become popular to refer to groups such as the American Green Berets and British SAS as "modern ninja," the label is nonetheless quite inappropriate for several reasons. The modern soldier, even a member of the so-called elite units, is restricted in his possibilities of action by national and international laws governing the waging of warfare. Certain actions and tactics are legally out of the question, even for the shadowy Delta Force operatives. Because the ninja families were viewed as outlaws by their oppressors from the beginning, nothing was considered as off-limits when it came down to protecting loved ones and homesteads. It should also be remembered that the modern soldier takes his orders from superiors who in turn take their orders from other superiors. The elite soldier is therefore limited to acting as the weapon of his government, and is discouraged from "interpreting" orders through the screen of his own political views and conscience.

The feudal ninja, on the other hand, had to combine three areas of expertise; he was required to be a physically adept combatant, a clever tactician and political operator, and his own philosopher and future-forecaster as well. Perhaps the most significant difference between the ninja and the modern elite unit soldier, however, is the fact that the ninja only went into action because he was forced to as a means of securing his homeland. He had no other choice except to surrender and submit to the wishes of his oppressors. The modern fighting man most often carries out his duties as a professional who is engaged in a chosen career. He is not forced to fight for survival; he selects his occupation from a wide range of possible choices.

- *Since all martial arts are similar, the outstanding feature of ninjutsu training is night stealth exercises.*

As a system of studying for the cultivation of martial prowess, virtue, and invincibility, the art of ninjutsu has no parallels today. Because of the societal roots of the ninja warrior tradition, there was never a "birth" or founding of the art of ninjutsu as there would have been for other more modern martial arts such as karate, judo, or aikido. Unlike the popular sports systems that first come to mind when hearing the term "martial arts," the warrior tradition of ninjutsu reaches back over a millennium of Japanese history to roots in combat survival in a world that seemed to know only war. As that original warfare survival method, the art that later came to be referred to as ninjutsu encompassed virtually every type of fighting skill that could be imagined as necessary to handle a killer enemy. Bare hands, bows and arrows, swords, explosives, battle-axes, spying methods, and castle fortifications were all studied for their benefits. No possible vulnerability was left unacknowledged.

It was only within the past 150 years of Japanese history that the once pragmatic and all-encompassing combat arts were fractioned and separated into individual and seemingly unrelated disciplines. The martial artist can now study the art of grappling without having to consider blades or kicks. One can study the art of drawing the sword without having to acknowledge arrows or arm locks. One can study the art of striking without having to enter into techniques for shooting a rifle or diving to the ground from horseback. Such systems of martial exclusivity are contrary to the spirit of the original ninja combat method, and therefore cannot form a basis, even in combination with other pieces of the warrior whole, for that which could possibly be taught as ninjutsu in name.

- *The ninja of old was the ultimate warrior in all aspects; incredibly conditioned fighting machine, intelligence expert, wilderness survivalist, chemist, priest, doctor, explosives technician, etc.*

Since the ninja families of feudal Japan were vastly outnumbered by their powerful enemies, they had to rely on far more than mere battlefield skills alone. Training covered the complete range of skills and tactics needed to survive in an incredibly hostile world. However, the truth is that no one person could actually master all of those disciplines, each one of which alone would require a lifetime study for mastery.

One of the tactics employed by the ninja was the cultivation of illusion as a means of thwarting an enemy. Since the ninja was an unknown adversary, a man of no name and no identity, it was a simple matter to create the illusion that the consummate skills of several different warriors and craftsmen were the work of a single ninja. In actual application, the ninja family would assign a team of experts in varied fields to complete the job that was perceived by others as being handled by a lone agent. Further, if all ninja were seen to be capable of such extremely refined and broad-reaching skills, the enemy was even more discouraged in his labor of trying to defeat the ninja families.

* *Because of the ninja's ability to call upon his training in the occult and supernatural, it is possible for him to defeat adversaries of greater speed, strength, and fighting prowess.*

The ninja's working knowledge of natural laws was based on his or her exposure to the concepts of mystical knowledge that found their fuller expression in the practices of mikkyo esoteric doctrines, *shugendo* (mountain cultivation of power), and related mind/body/spirit disciplines. In its legitimate practice, mysticism is the study of natural laws in their fullest, and embodies an approach to becoming the most fully developed human being possible.

In truth, the teachings of the ninja's mystical lore do not deal with anything "supernatural" at all. To the contrary, it is the intimate familiarization with the natural laws of the universe that make up the ninja's esoteric studies. This close-working familiarity with the principles of nature can, however, provide the mistaken impression that the ninja is somehow able to "bend" the laws and accomplish that which is beyond physical possibility.

Because of the ninja's heightened senses of awareness, and years of developmental training, it is sometimes possible for the ninja to actually move slower than his faster adversary and still defeat him through the sensitivity that permits perfect timing. Likewise, it is also possible for the ninja to defeat an attacker who generates superior muscle power. With effective body placement and timing, the larger attacker in effect knocks himself out by running into the fist of the defending ninja.

The realms of psychological perspective are as well areas for application of the ninja's occult teaching skills. Through growing familiarization with the psychological states that result from facing conflict and confrontation, the ninja learns how to read the intentions of others. As with the physical training of ninjutsu, this mental training as well focuses on developing heightened awareness; it is not a matter of learning "supernatural" or "unnatural" skills.

- *There are no true ninja in existence today.*

This is my favorite line found in a book referring to ninjutsu that was written by a respected American scholar of the Japanese martial arts. I say "favorite" because it is so typical of a whole set of martial artists who would do anything possible to avoid acknowledging the power and significance of what it is we have to offer the world. Apparently what that writer meant was that there are no longer any feudal Japanese survivalist clans living clandestine lives on pain of death if exposed in the mountains of south central Japan. I would not argue with that; what I would argue with is the writer's inappropriately narrow definition of ninjutsu.

All things grow and change with the passage of the centuries. It is no longer necessary to use the ninja arts against the governing powers that rule the Japanese nation. Therefore, the philosophies and methods of the once underground counterforce are no longer illegal. Persons wearing blue long-tailed coats and white-powdered wigs freezing in tiny log cabins at Valley Forge were once recognized as the Army of the struggling United States of America. Because U.S. infantrymen no longer wear such costumes in the 20th century, are we required to state that there is no true Army in existence today?

CHAPTER THREE

The sculpting artist
endeavors to remove only just enough rock
to free the desired image trapped within.
The martial artist
likewise works to let go of all limitations
that bar him from the freedom and power he seeks.

NINPO TAIJUTSU
Movement as art

The term "martial artist" is an interesting example of a commonly accepted usage of words that somehow does not accurately live up to the truth of the concept that it attempts to express. Contrary to the common usage of the term "martial artist," as used to describe a person training in the Oriental combat disciplines, true martial artists do not become artists until they have perfected the usage of their tools and have gone on to the level of pure spontaneous creativity. Therefore, the use of the word "artist" is in the vast majority of cases applied far too prematurely.

People accumulate skills that lead to the ability to generate works of art; artistic abilities are not merely acquired as a product of taking a course of instruction. A musician first learns how to make sounds mechanically and how to read music so that he can explore all possibilities. Eventually, pure creativity in an improvisation session earns him the reputation of being a musical artist. A painter first learns to pencil in perspective and shade colors mechanically so that he can eventually create works of art. Once he has transcended the mechanics, he can then enter the realm of pure self-expression through the medium of the graphic image.

Martial arts are no different. We accumulate experiences in technique and split-second decision-making that eventually lead to a level of ability that can be described by others as artistic. We cannot simply acquire martial artistry by enrolling in a course of study at the local martial arts school.

In its ultimate form as a guide to a way of living, the warrior path to enlightenment is a process of cultivating capabilities based on personally experienced insights, while at the same time letting go of negative limiting factors that hinder the openness and freedom that are required for advancement. Our martial arts is our method of approaching this process of transformation. We work and study and progress in the direction of becoming artists; we do not presuppose ourselves to be already worthy of the title by the mere fact that we are dressed in a martial training suit.

Approaching the Embodiment of Art

One of the first major mistakes that must be eliminated when moving from the limiting realm of martial hobbyist to the level of enlightenment martial artist is the insistence on momentarily freezing in place at the completion of each individual move in a string of combat actions and reactions. This deviation from the dynamics required to prevail in a real-life defensive encounter is often inappropriately labeled as "focus" in many of the modern (developed within the past 100 years) kick and punch martial systems. The tendency to break the flow of the fight into individual frozen sections of seemingly independent actions is perhaps understandable as a temporary gimmick to assist beginners with little experience to isolate and perfect specific movements that will later be blended back into a natural flow. When the masters of those systems insist on performing their techniques with the regularly timed freeze-pauses inserted between moves, however, it is more clearly an indication of lack of depth in understanding moving energy in a condition of confrontation than it is a matter of being merely a "different style" than the flow-oriented training methods.

This unreal abberation in training for possible real-world street or field survival is a major problem in the martial arts world today, in that two powerful forces continue to reinforce and restate this point-to-point method of movement that has no parallel whatsoever in the world of nature. These two forces work to distract martial practitioners from the reality they claim to seek, in that the mistake in all its bizarrely affected unnaturalness is presented as being "above," and therefore preferable to, the natural flow of movements as they occur in unself-conscious beings in nature.

The first factor contributing to the myth of freeze-frame action as being desirable is the popular glamorization of this method in the martial arts movies that regularly pull in great numbers of martial practitioners who wish to advance their own skills in the combat arts. What the viewers do not realize, however, is that escapist adventure films regularly rely on the *exaggeration* of the natural to excite audiences. Therefore, the hero of the martial art film is taken out of the limiting reality of true-life street combat and given what the producers consider to be an edge or an advantage that sets him apart from all the others. While the film's bad guys swing and lunge like lesser mortals, the hero carries himself magically through the carnage with a series of deft pose-strike-freeze pose-strike-freeze actions. Often, his face as well reflects this bizarre "statue comes to life and then returns to statue" approach to movement in a movie fight.

There is a natural follow-up phenomenon to this first factor contributing to the illusion that point-to-point action is the preferred way to handle a fight. If the screen heroes of the world's junior martial hopefuls dramatically defeat all their adversaries with whip-and-freeze stop action techniques, it is, of course, only natural for young martial tournament competitors to emulate their heroes when in the sports ring. The powerful urge to imitate is difficult if not impossible for the less than confident to overcome. Since the majority of people studying the martial arts in the Western world seem to get involved at least tangentially with teachers who relate to the competitive sport scene, it is highly unlikely that there would be any great popular shift away from the odd point-to-point grimace and tension dynamics that have somehow wormed their way into our culture as the accepted way to do things in the martial arts. Ironically enough in light of the facts behind why the martial arts were developed in the feudal ages of Japan, very few people today seem involved with or interested in pragmatic non-sport martial training methods. Therefore, the myth somehow lives on, growing stronger with every generation.

There is as well a second factor contributing to the prevalence of the freeze-frame tension approach to what in reality can only be experienced as a dynamic flow of projecting and receiving exchanges. In ages past, the only exposure a student could get to the martial arts was direct contact with a master technician. Whether actively studying that fighter's art or merely watching a demonstration of the techniques, personal contact was the only exposure one could have. Today, the majority of martial hopefuls find their first exposure to the martial arts through films, magazines or books. Many people even attempt to teach themselves the martial arts from books and magazines when they are not able to find access to a teacher that they respect. Since the printed medium is restricted to two-dimensional views and single-moment glimpses, it is difficult to experience anything having to do with timing on the printed page.

This chapter of this volume in this series of books then must work to further illuminate the proper way to take the mechanics of this martial system and bring them to life in the context of a vibrant, spontaneous, and fully self-expressing art form. This author must attempt the impossible by relating in static printed words and pictures the ultimate reality of freedom of choice in movement, and the blending of cause with effect that makes up the actual experience of street and field combat survival.

In the *Tao Te Ching,* the timeless and legendary volume of taoist lore attributed to the ancient Chinese sage Lao Tsu, it is said that "the tao" (universal process of the flow of all that is) that can be described is not the true tao." Likewise, any ultimate observation or discussion of the universe becomes an awkward impossibility because that very discussion itself can only be but a part of the vastness of the universe being described; it is not possible to move outside the universal process to observe that universe. Therefore, to describe a physical sensation such as proper movement dynamics in ninpo taijutsu through the printed media is as frustrating as trying to pin down the tao or step outside the universe for an outsider's view.

Body Attitudes

There are, however, some natural places to begin a look at how to interpret and embody the ability to capture and become part of that natural flow that characterizes the ninja's approach to handling all opposition in life. Perhaps the most obvious place to begin is a look at the *kamae* (fighting attitudes) of the ninja's taijutsu combat method.

Someone once wrote that emotion could be thought of as "e-motion," or "energy in motion." That is a perfect way to describe the kamae fighting postures of ninpo taijutsu. Not poses, postures, or stances as such, the kamae are better described as bodily manifestations of our emotional processes as they flow from one second to the next. Through the kamae, we enact in the exterior world those privately observed needs that come into being and well up in our own interior world.

Properly assumed under the pressure of self-protection combat, the kamae does not at all need to be remembered; it is a totally natural and spontaneous phenomenon. If I am feeling overwhelmed, I just naturally tend to want to draw my body back and away from the danger. In the ninja's taijutsu training, we call this action of pulling the body trunk away from the attack the *ichimonji no kamae.* If I feel that stopping an attack before it builds its momentum is the only way to handle the current situation, I just naturally tend to want to move in close to my adversary where I can take control of him. In our training hall, we call this action of sending the body trunk forward into building danger the *jumonji no kamae.*

The kamae of the ninja fighting arts are in truth actions. They are movements and not static stances. The kamae should not be thought of as poses, although the words "pose" or "posture" are used occasionally in my books for the sake of convenience in describing verbally the actions experienced in the physical world. As actions, the kamae come into being as our thought processes spontaneously mold our bodies into the form needed from within, based on the growing perception of the demands of external reality. Therefore, the kamae need not be remembered once the training process has come into flower. The kamae just *happen* as they are needed, and leave the body frame as they are no longer appropriate.

Because the kamae are summoned up as they are needed, it is not necessary to think ahead and assume the kamae as a pose before the action comes into being. New students often do not understand this concept, and express their doubts and uncertainties with misbased questions such as, "What if I am attacked before I have time to get into my fighting stance?" The ninja does not need to be in any set stance or posture before the attack. The kamae is assumed as the attack from an adversary begins to unfold. Therefore, assuming the kamae is an actual part of the protective action itself.

In the following examples, the kamae are shown coming into manifestation as the action of the confrontation develops. Note that the kamae are *not* assumed as static postures or stances before the energy of the conflict erupts into fighting action.

Ichimonji no Kamae
(Defensive Posture)

(1-3) The defender drops back away from the potential damage delivered by the aggressor's first attack.

(4&5) As the second punch is thrown, the defender shifts again to allow the punch to miss its intended

Continued

target. (6) The attacker grabs the defender's left wrist. (6A) The *ichimonji no kamae* is assumed as the defender then takes control of his attacker's actions. Using an arm bar to the attack-

er's right arm, (7-11) the defender goes on to use the aggressor's own motions against him, twisting the attacker's left arm under his own right arm, and bringing him down.

1

2

**Doko no Kamae
(Responsive Posture)**

(1-5) The defender moves alongside the aggressor's attack, slips past the punch, and (5A) assumes a *doko no*

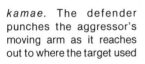
kamae. The defender
punches the aggressor's
moving arm as it reaches
out to where the target used

Continued

6

7

to be. (6-11) The defender then applies a *mushadori* (arm scoop elbow lock) to capture the attacker's left arm and lead him into sub-

8

9

mission. Note the defender's use of body motion to lead the adversary into positions of unbalance.

10

11

Jumonji no Kamae
(Offensive Posture)

In this example of a possible fight scenario, the defender (1&2) responds to his attacker's advance with a commited forward action. (3) Angling his advance so as to avoid the attacker's leading hand punch, the defender counterpunches into the adversary's arm from the (3A)

forward moving *jumonji no ka-mae.* A left leading arm slam (4), a right cross punch, and then (5) a left leading hand punch are driven into the attacker's arm to move him into a position from which it is difficult for him to continue forward. (6) The defender then

41

Continued

7

8

executes an upward hooking leap kick to fold the attacker, and a (7-12) leaping down-

9

ward stomp kick to the knee to
down his larger adversary.

Hoko no Kamae
(Evasive Posture)

From close range, (1&2) the aggressor moves in with a short strong hook punch to the defender's head. (3) Rather than attempt to stop his stronger assailant, the defender instead shifts evasively to the inside of the attacker's punch. (3A) While he moves, the defender as-

sumes the *hoko no kamae* and executes a right forearm slam to the attacker's head. The defender simultaneously pins the attacker's left fist against the attacker's chest with his right forearm. The defender immediately (4&5) shifts

Continued

5

back to his left to avoid a possible left follow-up punch from the attacker. He maintains forearm pressure on the attacker's face the entire time. (6) Continuing

6

on around the attacker, the defender advances with his right leg to form a tripping fulcrum over which (7-9) he throws his adversary to the ground.

1

Hicho no Kamae
(Single Leg Posture)

(1-3) The defender intercepts the aggressor's front kick with a stamping heel kick of

2

his own. (4&5) The attacker
continues with a wrist grab

Continued

and (6&7) a second kick. The defender shifts out of the way of the second kick while applying a rising knee strike to the underside of the attacker's extended leg. (7A) From the *hicho no kamae* the defender (8) steps in the

direction of the momentum of the attacker's kick, trapping both his leg and arm with the same move. (9-11) From his unbalanced position, the attacker is then easy to force to the ground.

Hira no Kamae
(Receiving Posture)
Example One

(1&2) The defender's sleeve is grabbed by an attacker. Rather than attempt to deal with the entangled arm, the defender instead uses (3&4) turning body momentum to

3

propel his left forearm into the right side of the attacker's head. (5) The defender continues to turn, stepping forward with his left foot into a (5A) *hira no kamae*

4

5A

5

Continued

6

which (6&7) flings the attacker to the ground. Continuing to permit the attacker to maintain his grip on his sleeve, (8-10) the defender

7

54

positions himself so that his right knee props up the attacker's right arm while his left knee exerts painful downward pressure.

**Hira no Kamae
Example Two**

(1) In this example, two aggressors confront the single defender. (2) One attacker grabs the defender's wrist to hold him in place for a punch. (3) The defender responds by shifting to his right suddenly and (4) using his body weight in motion to

carry his trapped arm into the face of the second attacker. (4A) Assuming the *hira no kamae* as he moves, the defender (5&6) is able to use his body motion to unbalance the two attackers against one another and throw them to the ground.

Seiza
(Grounded Posture)

(1) The defender is grabbed from behind. (2) He leans forward and then (3) snaps his head back to strike the attacker in the face with a stunning blow. (4&5) The defender

Continued

then kicks forward, (6) swinging both legs upward to build momentum for a (7&8) downward leg swing that brings the defender to the ground on his knees. From the stability of this (8A) *seiza,* the defender (9&10) captures the attacker's forward staggering motion and propels him over on his back.

Dakentaijutsu Striking Skills

"A punch is a punch," it has been said. At an ultimate level, that is of course true. Getting to the point where your body demonstrates that truth as a natural and unconscious way of moving, however, does take some work.

Like many people, you may have begun your martial arts training with a basic ability to ball up your hand, tighten your shoulder, and hurl your fist with accuracy toward a target. The more you examine this basic self-developed skill, however, the more small flaws you might uncover. Thus begins the training phase where a punch is studied for the details that will make it a more effective tool. Many martial artists are a bit dismayed to find that their punching skills actually deteriorate a bit during this phase, due to the temporary heavy emphasis placed on intellectually monitoring the small subtle actions that make up the response and delivery of that process that we label a "punch." Eventually, the new realizations discovered become internalized, and the punch once again returns to its original unself-conscious position in your arsenal of usable self-protection tools.

As a scientific way of going about learning to punch effectively, you first need to understand a few structural principles. Then you have to work at developing the physical skills that properly embody those principles. In other words, first you have to understand how to do it, then you have to develop the ability to actually put what you know into action. Real development can only come once you have had a chance to integrate an intellectual understanding of the "tricks" that allow the mechanics to work on a purely physical level.

Standard punching dynamics fundamentals can be broken down for examination into a series of three ranges, three angles of impact, three height levels, and three methods of delivery dynamics.

The three ranges include targets for which you must extend your reach, targets within natural easy reach, and targets so close as to cause you to shorten your natural reach.

The three angles of impact include inward hooking, direct forward piercing, and outward swatting.

The three heights include targets that require you to reach above your shoulder, relatively level with your shoulder, and below your shoulder—high, middle, and low levels (*jodan, chudan,* and *gedan* in Japanese).

The three methods of delivery mechanics include punching with your leading hand, punching with your rear hand (the cross punch), and punching with what begins as your rear hand and becomes your leading hand as you lunge forward with a step during the punch.

From this collection of possibilities, 81 different combinations of heights, distancing, dynamics, and angling can be put together from this most basic grouping of 12 components. Many students could feel that the thought of consistently drilling 81 different strikes with both right and left hands is more than a bit intimidating or even discouraging, however. Therefore, temporarily concentrating on being aware of these 12 basic working components is an excellent place to begin your intellectual study of the mechanics of punching, which you will then take on to personalization through repetition of punching drills.

The following examples demonstrate possible *fudoken* forefist punches embodying combinations from the list of 12 fundamental components.

The following three technique series illustrate the three ranges of reach. Each of the three actions employs a similar straight right cross punch for purposes of illustration.

1

2

Long Range

In this first series, (1-4) the defender executes a middle

level long-range, rear hand cross, straight piercing punch.

Middle Range

In this second series, (1-4) the defender executes a

lower level, middle-range, rear hand cross, straight piercing punch.

1

Close Range

In this third series, (1-3) the defender executes a lower level, close-range, rear hand cross, straight piercing punch.

69

The following three series illustrate the three angles of impact. Each of the three actions employs a similar middle-range, leading hand, upper level punch for purposes of illustration.

Inward Hooking

In this first series, (1-4) the defender executes an upper level, middle-range, leading

3

hand inward, hooking punch into his adversary's moving right arm.

4

1

2

Outward Swatting

In this second series, (1-4) the defender executes an upper level, middle-range, leading hand outward, swat-

ting punch against his adversary's right hand speed jab.

1

2

Direct Forward Piercing

In this third series, (1-4) the defender demonstrates an upper level, middle-range, leading hand direct forward,

piercing punch into the
adversary's right hand
speed jab.

Shoulder height is used as the standard of judgment. Targets more or less level with the shoulder are considered middle level targets. Below shoulder height are the lower level targets, and above shoulder height are the high level targets.

1

2

Middle Level

This series shows a combination of two middle level long-range forward piercing punches. The first of the two punches, (1-3) a left leading

3

hand strike, is directed at the adversary's upraised left guard arm. (4) After the impact of the initial punch, the

4

Continued

5

6

adversary (5&6) attempts to counterattack with a right punch. The adversary's punch is (7&8) jammed however, by means of a quickly executed right cross punch into the adversary's moving right forearm. Note the defender's reliance on body shifting to place himself safely in a position to avoid possible counter punches. The body moving through space on flexing knees also serves to generate additional power for the punches.

7

8

1

2

Lower Level

This series embodies a principle similar to that demonstrated in the previous example. In this case however, the defender (1-3) executes a lower level inward hooking

left leading punch to the adversary's left cross punch attack. The defender then (4&5) follows up with a right shoulder-level mid-range straight punch to the head.

1

2

High Level

This series of actions demonstrates a high level of long-range rear-to-front lunging inward hooking punch. The defender (1-4) moves from a left forward

3

posture to a right forward posture while delivering a quick right hand hook punch to the adversary's up-raised right guard arm.

4

Here, instead of the punch, the kick is used as an example to not only illustrate the three methods of delivery but also to remind the reader that these delivery dynamics apply to both punching and kicking.

Lead

The defender is (1&2) attacked by an adversary who comes forward with an intended kick. (3) The defender applies a *sokuyaku* kick with his lead leg to the as-

sailant's lower leg to effectively stop his aggressive technique. (4) The defender's lead leg remains in the lead as he steps down.

1

Cross

Here the defender again (1-5) applies a bottom-of-the-foot stamp kick to the adversary's midsection. In this case, however, what begins

2

as the rear leg is retained in a rear position, resulting in a cross body kick similar in principle to the cross punch.

Cross and Forward Step

In this application of the heel kick, the defender (1-4) pulls his knee high and (5&6) sends the sole of his foot into the adversary's midsec-

tion to knock him backwards. What was the defender's rear leg becomes his leading leg in the course of this technique.

Natural Striking Tools

The ninja warrior's *ninpo taijutsu dakenjutsu* (striking methods) employ a fundamental arsenal of natural body weapons known as the *juroppoken* (16 body striking tools). As a place to begin your training, whether for *koppojutsu* (bone attacking) methods or *koshijutsu* (muscle and organ) attacks, the basic tools can be listed as follows:

Kikakuken Zutsuki: Head butt

Taiken Katatsuki: Right and left shoulder slam

Shukiken: Right and left elbow smash

Fudoken: Right and left clenched fist strike

Taiken Dembutsuki: Right and left hip slam

Sokkiken: Right and left knee strike

Sokuyaku: Right and left bottom of foot stamp

Sokugyaku: Right and left toe drive kick

Shizenken: Total body weapon variations. In addition to the more common weapons associated with unarmed combat, there is as well the option of using any part of the body if it serves the overall purpose. Shizenken include an infinite collection of strikes and hits from all parts of the body. Shin strikes, shoulder shoves, hip slams, and bites are all possibilities of self-defense tools from the ninja's shizenken classification.

With 81 different types of single hits (based on combinations of the 12 components) to practice from both left and right sides as applied with each of the ninpo taijutsu juroppoken, the student of the *kihon* (fundamentals) has a total of 1,296 basic kinds of strikes to practice *just to get started.* Beyond that comes lots of drills to personalize and internalize the striking skills.

1

2

Kikakuken Zutsuki
(Head Butt Smash)

The defender, though (1) held in place by his adversary, still has the freedom to (2) apply a *zutsuki* to the face. Note that the defender uses crouching knees, rather than a torso hunching action, to position and deliver the strike.

Taiken Katatsuki
(Shoulder Slam)

The shoulder is an underrated weapon in many scientific combat teaching systems. Here, the defender uses his left shoulder to (1&2) strike and deflect the attacker's right leading hand punch. The defender then quickly shifts on his feet to drive his right shoulder into the attacker's face as the attacker attempts a left follow-up punch.

Shukiken
(Elbow Slam)

To defend himself against an incoming roundhouse kick, the defender (1) shifts inside the radius of the circular kick and allows the kicker's momentum to supply the power for a (2&3) *shukiken* to the face.

2

3

1

**Fudoken
(Forefist)**

Proper body positioning allows the defender to (1) respond aggressively to the attacker's front kick without

2

3

the necessity of blocking first. (2-4) A *fudoken* punch stops the attacker's forward momentum.

4

**Taiken Dembutsuki
(Hip Slam)**

Even the hip can be used as an effective punching weapon. Here, (1&2) the defender drops his weight onto the assailant's forward leg, using his hip to straighten and then (3) damage the attacker's trapped knee.

2

3

Sokkiken
(Knee Strike)

(1&2) The *sokkiken* is applied against an immobilized elbow joint to free the defender from an attacker's grab. Note that the defender uses his entire body to apply the strike, rather than merely popping his knee into place and back.

Sokuyaku
(Heel Kick)

When grabbed from behind, the defender uses an upward hooking *sokuyaku* to the adversary's groin. The defender (1) first leans slightly forward to unbalance his attacker before (2&3) shifting into his single-legged kicking position.

Sokugyaku
(Toe Stab Kick)

The defender (1-4) uses *sokugyaku* to reduce the fighting capabilities of his adversary. Note the flexed knee and solid footing of the de-

fender's ground leg. This allows the kicking leg to deliver maximum power to its target.

CHAPTER FOUR

You are indeed worth defending.
There are those whose love you share
*   those whose days brighten with your presence*
*   those who count on you.*
Just how much
*   are you willing to do*
*   in order to assure*
*   that the twisted actions of the perverse*
*   do not destroy the joy*
*   in the hearts of those you love?*

JISSEN NO HO

Self-defense fighting

Before beginning my training in the Japanese tradition of ninjutsu, I studied with a martial arts instructor who advocated that his art was only ten percent physical and fully 90 percent mental when it came to street self-defense. By this statement, that instructor meant to imply that all the technique in the world would still be found to be lacking if the martial artist was unable to summon up and engage the proper frame of mind and fighting spirit when it came time to face a murderous attacker.

This grim reality is indeed even more appropriate to acknowledge in this age of "enforced peace" in which we all live. Just where do we go to get our lessons in cultivating this all-important "90 percent" that hovers above training in mechanical technique itself? How are students of the fighting arts to know if their teachers and lessons are valid and are taking them progressively toward the twin goals of confidence and safety that so often inspire citizens of the modern world to seek out the study of the arts of self-protection?

It is common for instructors of the formalized martial sports and recreation systems so popular in the world today to assume that because they are skilled in their system's set way of performing basic movements, *kata*, steps, strikes, and throws, they are automatically qualified to discuss and give expert instruction in self-defense and street-combat survival. This often completely false assumption is made despite the fact that the majority of popular martial arts available in the world today did not have their foundings based on the premise of self-protection combat. Most of today's martial arts were established either as sports or spiritual development systems; their founders did not intend for them to be used as methods for streetfighting. In truth, the majority of martial systems popularly offered to customers today are nowhere near being related to the cold and often horrible realities of self-protection combat.

It could be argued that there is only one truly reliable way to become a master of the technique of fighting other people. Facetiously of course, I offer the following suggestions as to how to become good at fighting.

First of all, find a place where you are sure to encounter people who fit the following categories:

• They all feel deprived of many of the benefits that life has presented others (financially, culturally, racially, politically, etc.), and resent those others as actually being less deserving than they themselves, even though those others live more satisfying lives.

• They all experience inner annoyance and lack of fulfillment as a result of agitated internal electrochemical imbalances (inability to attain a sufficient level of satiation for sexual demands or proper nutritional balance).

• They all blur any possible realization of personal social and community responsibilities by inculcating reduced powers of discretion, discernment, and rational thought through the intentional abuse of intoxicating substances.

In other words, the first major step in this procedure of learning how to be a tough fighter is to find a low-class pick-up bar.

The second step is to enter the bar and shove some of the patrons around, either verbally or physically.

The third step is to experience the action of the fight.

The fourth step is to check out of the hospital and wait for the next weekend so that you can repeat the process all over again.

Continue to follow these four steps until you have gained sufficient experience to enable you to eliminate the necessity of going through the fourth step every time.

Perhaps the ultimate in efficient and effective methods for developing the skill of defeating other people in fights is to arrange to be born into a family that dwells in the heart of a violent and deprived community, and lacks the collective education to understand the mechanics of how fear, cruelty, violence, disease, and ignorance perpetuate themselves from one generation to the next. After growing up hungry, abused, and frustrated, by the time you reach young adulthood you will undoubtedly be a good fighter if you survive the training of your youth.

What of training for those persons who were not born in the inhumane realms of hatred, aggression, abusive greed, intolerance, and ignorance? How are those persons who were born in realms of peace, fulfillment, joy, and enlightened growth to go about cultivating the combat self-protection skills necessary for survival when forced to enter the darker, less elevated strata of human society?

Here are some practical suggestions for cultivating fighting spirit without going so far as to poison your positive outlook on life in general:

• *Be honest about your feelings.* Recognize and acknowledge those emotions that could save you in a confrontation as they appear in your consciousness. Do not back down from rightful anger in the face of danger just because you were culturally patterned to be a "good little child" 30 years ago. Muggers, thieves, and rapists often count on their potential victims to be "good and moral citizens," unwilling to resort to the same kind of brutal and unsocial violence that the criminal chooses to direct at them.

• *Be aware.* Do not allow yourself to travel through life as though encased in a narrow envelope of fog. Actively expand the scope of your senses. Whenever you catch yourself drifting or pulling in your awareness when you are out in a public place, firmly remind yourself that that is not what you are training to do and return your conscious perception out to your surroundings once again. Remember that this will take time and work, so do not let yourself get discouraged if past bad habits are tough to shake off.

• *Listen to your hunches.* Do not venture into situations that you feel somehow have a high percentage of probability of turning into dangerous confrontations. If you are not sure of yourself in a certain situation, why take a chance unnecessarily? Find a safer, more reliable way to get done what you must do.

• *Be creative.* Do not think that conventional fist fighting must always be the answer when confronted by a hostile assailant. Sometimes it is possible to confuse your attacker so that he does not see you as the victim, sometimes you can disappear from the dangerous situation, and sometimes you can set up an inescapable trap from which your assailant cannot get at you.

• *Know your own powers and limitations.* Long before you find yourself in a physical confrontation, take the time to explore the various things you can and cannot do. With knowledgable friends or a qualified martial arts instructor, try out your basic strikes and kicks, body shifts and dodges, and grabs or throws. Find out what you are best at doing and hone those skills into useable form. Find out what you are weakest at doing and either train diligently to build up those skills, or be especially careful to avoid situations where those weak points will have to be faced.

• *Plan ahead.* Practice with realistic drills just exactly what you will say, think, and do in the case of an actual attack. Do not waste your time trying to develop fancy exotic technique skills like you see in the movies. Do not confuse tactics for winning martial arts contests with life-protecting combat skills; streetfights rarely ever resemble sports tournaments. Stick to realistic and reliable basic moves that have a lesser chance of going wrong. Use your meditation sessions to rehearse mentally just what you will do in those scenarios most likely to happen in your own life. Have your strategy planned out so that you are not forced to think everything through in a time of extreme pressure and danger.

• *Be appropriate.* Honestly acknowledge just what the purpose of self-defense is all about. Keep in mind that your goal is to get home in a safe and healthy manner. Do not get fooled or pressured into feeling that you are obligated in any way to handle the confrontation in a set manner. In a life-threatening self-defense situation, you are not at all obliged to win a fighting contest, convert a criminal mind to morally enlightened behavior, prove how special you are, clean up the streets for other potential victims, embody ideal macho movie hero behavior, or do anything at all beyond not being killed or maimed. If you can acknowledge this in a sincere and from-the-heart manner, you can create a lot more room for potential actions other than a toe-to-toe hook and jab fist fight. You can see that running, trickery, "dirty" tactics, "unfair" fighting techniques, or anything at all that comes to mind or hand is a valid means for getting home in a safe and healthy condition.

• *Be realistic.* Do not kid yourself about just how far you would be willing to go in a self-defense confrontation. It is easy to talk tough about all you will do if assaulated, and yet quite another situation when the events suddenly bring a human being against you as an attacker. Will you really be able to go through with all the violent actions that you can so easily describe in theory? If your response to any discussion of self-protection is, "I'll just rely on my trusty .45 automatic," are you truly willing to draw and fire no matter what the attack, and are you really willing to stand up and take the legal consequences resulting from such action?

• *Keep in touch with local events.* Check newspapers, listen to the radio, watch TV news, and keep on the alert for information concerning local trends in personal attacks in your community, or in areas that you may be traveling to visit. Take appropriate cautions and plan ahead so that you are not caught off-guard by something that you could have known about ahead of time.

• *Use everything at hand!* A self-defense situation is nothing at all like a sports competition. An attacker will easily use your hesitation to resort to "unfair" tactics as an aid to accomplishing his own lowly intentions. Therefore, cultivate a mind set of doing whatever it takes to guarantee your safety.

Self-Defense
Example One

In this scenario, (1) an assailant confronts the defender with a clothing grab choke. (2) The defender responds with a palm heel strike to the attacker's face, which sets up the momentum for (3-6) a rear hip throw. Note that the defender uses walking steps, not jerking motions or upper-body strength alone, to unbalance the adversary and complete the throw.

Self-Defense
Example Two

It is important to use body momentum to confuse an attacker's sense of balance and control in a fight. Here, (1) an attacker grabs the defender's wrist in an attempt to hold him in place for a (2) punch or kick. The defender (3) quickly shifts back and then forward while rolling and straightening his captured arm to reverse the control back against the grabber. (4-7) Once wedged into an arm bar hold, the assailant is held in place by the defender's action of grabbing the fabric of his trouser leg with his left barring hand.

1

4

5

2

3

6

7

Self-Defense
Example Three

(1) Here the defender is grabbed by both arms. He responds by (2) moving toward his attacker and (3&4) around to the side. The sudden move causes the attacker to hold on to the defender's arms even tighter in a desperate attempt to retain control. By relying on body placement, the defender ends up in a position to (5-7) guide the attacker's strength against itself, driving the attacker's face down and into the defender's knee.

Self-Defense
Example Four

As much as possible, train to utilize whatever is thrown at you as an assist, rather than a hindrance. In this scenario, (1&2) the assailant suddenly turns a pointing finger into a head grab, taking the defender by surprise.

3

The defender (3&4) uses the attacker's movement to his advantage, however, ducking under, and emerging along the outside of the aggressor's grabbing left arm, using it as a shield. The de-

4

Continued

fender then (5) rises with a palm heel strike and eye jab, and continues through with

(6-8) an immediate knee lock sweep takedown to throw the attacker to the ground.

1

Self-Defense
Example Five

In this case, (1) the defender is grabbed by an attacker as he attempts to defuse the assailant's anger. In the process, (2) the defender's hand is grabbed and his fingers bent backward (see 2A). Rather than resist the surprise attack with tension moves, the defender goes with the force of the assault and allows his body position

2A

2

to accommodate the attacker's intentions. By (3) stepping forward with his free side, the defender alters his angle to remove the attacker's leverage advantage and take control of the attacker's body (see 3A). From the attacker's position of unbalance, it is then a natural process to (4&5) further pull him

Continued

over and off his feet. (6-9) A
swinging kick into the

straightened elbow of the
aggressor finishes the fight.

Self-Defense
Example Six

Of course, the "handshake trap" is one of the most common of aggressive body capture techniques. Here, (1&2) an attacker grabs the defender's hand and applies a crushing grip. The defender (3) guides the attacker's arm out and away, momentarily reducing the aggressor's leverage. The defender then (4) immediately shifts forward with a *zutsuki* head butt strike, making no effort to extract his trapped hand, and (5) jams the assailant's elbow into his lower abdomen. (6&7) Crouching on his own knees, the defender then trips the attacker onto his back, where he is subdued with an arm bar control and a descending knee to the head.

1

4

5

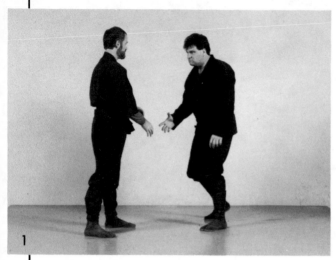

Self-Defense
Example Seven

Here, (1-3) the assailant's grab temporarily overpowers the defender. (4&5) The

defender uses a strike to the face as a distraction to al-

127 Continued

low him to (6) shift his body position slightly. As the attacker recovers and reapplies his force, (7) he is surprised to find that the defender's body has moved backward (the key is to move with a subtle knee flex) and is no longer susceptible to the same dynamics as used previously.

When the attacker applies his pulling force, (8) he unwittingly pulls himself forward into an arm trap. He supplies the power to unbalance his own body all by himself. (9-11) The defender then uses his own body weight in a straight drop downward to damage the assailant's wrist (see 11A).

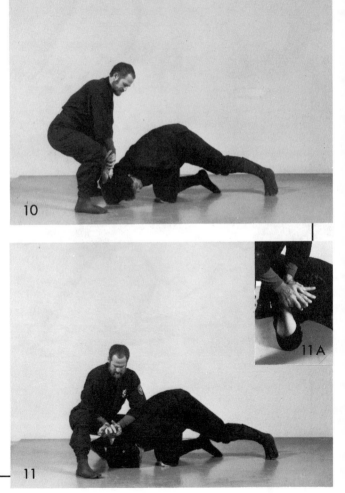

Self-Defense
Example Eight

In the scenario pictured here, (1) the defender is surprised by an attacker who suddenly produces a knife and charges. The defender (2) assumes a covering position, and then (3) captures the assailant's attacking motion with his hand and leg. (4) A looping swing kick bars the aggressor's arm and drives him face-first into the ground.

Self-Defense
Example Nine

(1) The grounded defender has his leg grabbed by an aggressor. (2&3) The defender relies on the attacker's strong left hand grip

2A

2

and circles his foot over and to the outside of the attacker's arm (see insets). (4) Wedging his foot beneath the attacker's arm, the de-

Continued

fender (5) uses the tense resistance in the attacker's
body as a tool for his defeat.
He (6&7) traps the attacker's

left leg to prevent him from recovering his balance as he (8) pulls him down by his trapped arm.

7

8

**Self-Defense
Example Ten**

(1-6) A similar technique can be used to counter a grab from the assailant's right

arm. The defender makes a
big sweeping loop with his

137 Continued

7

8

trapped leg, and then (7-12) applies a tripping action with his left leg once the at-

9

10

tacker begins to lose his
balance to bring him down.

11

12

1

Self-Defense
Example Eleven

The assailant (1&2) attacks the downed defender with an ankle-wrenching foot twist. (3) The defender goes with the force and allows his body to flip over with the at-

2

3

tacker's exertion. As he rolls over to accommodate the pain, (4&5) the defender entwines his free leg around the support leg of the unsus-

4

5

Continued

pecting attacker. (6-10) As the defender continues to roll, the attacker is levered

off balance and thrown to
the ground.

143

A

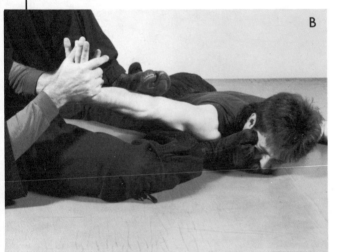

B

Stretching Arm Bars

These stretching arm bars (A-C) rely on leg extension to work the trapped limb into a position of control.

C

144

Straightened Levered Arm Bars

Here you may use either (A) the flattened palm or (B) the sole of the foot to apply pressure.

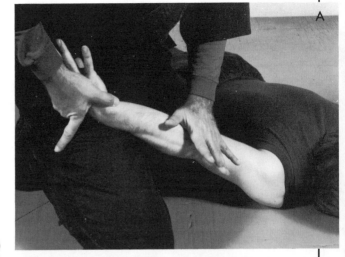

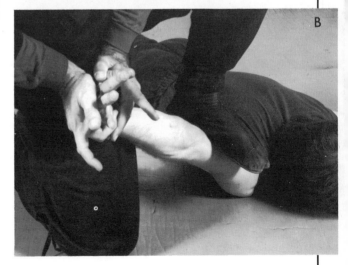

A

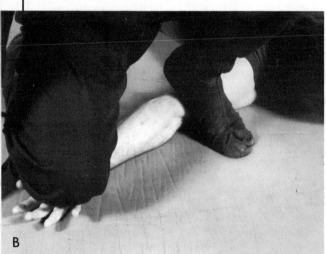

B

Crushing Arm Bars

(A&B) Employ the ground beneath the assailant's body as a tool for control.

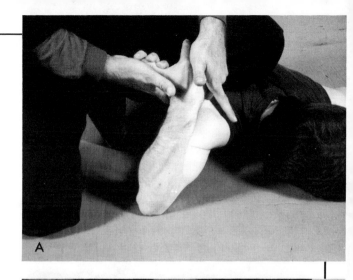

Limb Twists and Shears

These (A-C) are applied against an immovable limb using the ground as a base.

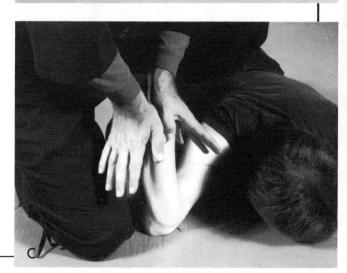

AFTERWORD

An interview with Stephen K. Hayes

This interview with Stephen K. Hayes, author of Ohara Publication's ninja book series, has been included in this fifth volume to offer readers further personal insights into the work of the author. The rather pointed questions and their sometimes controversial answers were compiled from a series of sessions conducted at Hayes' personal training hall.

Q. *This is not exactly the impression I had expected to find at the personal training hall of the man who introduced the practice of authentic ninjutsu to the Western world. A huge unmarked barn in a tiny Midwestern town; no sign whatsoever to help people find the place, and that limousine you pulled up in! Somehow, I feel that this is not what the world would imagine when they hear the word "ninja."*
A. You are right, absolutely right. But then, despite all the ninja movies, books, articles, and now, training halls all over the place, the cold fact remains that very, very few people in the world know anything at all about the authentic ninja legacy.

Q. *Then why the training hall with no sign? If you are concerned with changing the image of the art, I would think you would make it easier for people to find your training hall.*

A. Actually, at this stage of my personal career, I am not concerned with changing anything. My training hall is here for my own training. I do teach the senior teachers of the art in here, too, and they don't need a sign to find the place. There is no regular training for the public at this location.

Q. *How would an interested potential student go about learning the art from you?*

A. We (Shadows of Iga Society) offer seminars around the world. That would be a great place to start. There are, as well, dojo operated by my senior students where people can train full-time. Right now I am not set up to offer ongoing training to new people. Sometimes I just lock up the place and leave the country for months at a time to work with one of my teachers. Perhaps in the future I will change all this, when I am more prepared to settle down and teach others. I would like that eventually.

Q. *You use the word "warrior" very often. It is hard to imagine someone like Miyamoto Musashi, Japan's classic wandering warrior, traveling in a chauffered silver limousine like you do. Is that part of the false ninja stereotype, too?*

A. (Laughing). Sure is, especially if it bothers you. Look at it logically. Warrior training involves the cultivation of the ability to operate powerfully in any environment. Think about what that means. I have to be able to generate effortlessly any of the symbols or forms that charactertize anyone's concept of what embodies true power. I can live off the land as an effortless part of nature. I enjoy that power. But if that is all I can do, if I am helpless when it comes to moving in that part of the world that demands personal contacts and adequate financial resources, I am only half warrior and half weakling. Of course the opposite is true as well. I may be the wealthiest man on Wall Street, but I will still die like a beggar if I am unable to fit in with the natural elements in a survival or personal attack situation. Total capability is the goal of the warrior.

Q. *I had never thought of the art of ninjutsu in that light.*

A. The stereotype does get in people's way. Because I am trained as a ninja, some folks want to think of me as living under a rock someplace, only emerging at night to creep away and murder someone. Even some of my own students in the past could not handle their views of my life-style. They fret that I was too materialistic, too jet set, to be an authentic ninja warrior. That was their limited vision, of course.

Other friends shake their heads at me from the opposite perspective. They think I am crazy whenever I leave behind my so-called comforts. They ask why would I choose going out half-naked stalking imaginery enemies in the woods in the middle of winter instead of a warm bed at home. Where was that car and that house when I was sleeping in a dirt-floored shed in south central Tibet, just so I could scramble up the mountain at Tingri to talk with the one fighter monk who somehow avoided execution by the Communist Chinese when they attacked his monastery in 1959?

I love the diversity of my life. I love the fullness. I enjoyed being with the monk and his young disciples on the dirt floor when I was there and I enjoyed speaking with celebrities in the back of my limousine when I was there, too. It is the ninja mind set. Anywhere we are is, *just has to be,* great.

Q. *Is this ninja mind set a part of what you teach your students, the few who can find your unmarked barn dojo?*

A. No, it is not really appropriate for most of the people studying the art right now. This is a little awkward for me to discuss; I do not want to offend feelings here by appearing to be talking down to people, but actually what I am talking about is advanced training in ninjutsu. It is what my teachers want me to explore right now. Maybe we could say that it is not as necessary, there are more important matters, for newer students in the art.

Q. *Then would you say that your work with your Japanese and Tibetan master teachers at this point centers completely on the higher mental and spiritual aspects of the warrior traditions?*

A. I have found that I cannot really split my training up into compartments like that. By gaining complete control of my body through *taijutsu* (ninja unarmed combat) training, I eliminate those unconscious actions and interferences that prevent me from being open to the subtle influences that people refer to as mental or spiritual power. By studying to understand the ethereal higher laws of the universe, I gain new insights that facilitate totally effective employment of the physical realm. The goal is to experience balanced growth on all fronts.

It is tempting, I know, for students to see this art in one of two exaggerated extreme lights. On one extreme is the image of the ninja as the gritty and physical loner Rambo, blowing up Southeast Asia. On the other hand, other students want to see the ninja as the ethereal and magical wizard Obi Wan Kenobi casting spells to control the minds of enemies. The authentic art emphasizes balance in life and personal responsibility at all levels of living. Therefore, I must caution all students against seeing the various aspects of this art as being separate. We develop spiritual power by coming to grips with the details of physical reality. We gain control of the physical world by cultivating spiritual insight. This reality of the interpenetration of the two realms cannot be escaped. It is just that we choose to emphasize the physical in the beginning years of ninja training. We have to. There is no other way.

Q. *Well, I have read that there is a bit of controversy surrounding your art's emphasis on what some people refer to as "mystical elements." Is there a religious side of your art, and if so, are all students required to get involved with the ninja spiritual practice?*

A. In actuality, the so-called mystical elements really are not that mysterious at all. As I deal with these teachings, they are presented in a way that permits the student to learn to become aware of the truth that any action they perform has ramifications on several levels. Sure, a stab is just a stab, but there is much more to it if one is willing to look. Why is it that some persons are so much more effective than others in a fighting situation, or even in the real world of everyday life, even when those others might actually be stronger or train harder? I believe it has to do with the ability to observe the significance of several planes or shadings of reality with the same glance; a physical reality, an emotional reality, an interactive energy reality, a point in the unfolding of history reality, and many more beyond these obvious ones. If one can observe and be aware of these multiple views of reality, it is a simple and natural step to move right on to learning how to interpret and apply one's awareness as a means of generating desired results.

I am in no way teaching a religion, an occult hex, invisible power, or voodoo sort of thing, *as opposed to* physical training. Many times this has been misunderstood. People want to label me as either physical or spiritual, as though the two could be separated. Sometimes people look at the incredibly effective physical combat methods that have been researched and handed down over the centuries by the ancestors of our lineage, and say "yes, that looks great but when are we going to get to the energy channeling part?" It is not a matter of choosing one over the other, of being physical or being spiritual. Everything begins with the body. The so-called energy channeling or *kuji-in* (esoteric finger weaving of the ninja) aspects then heighten or broaden the practitioner's overall capabilities.

Therefore, the first step toward spiritual power is to become master of your own body. The first lesson in the mystical aspects of the art comes on the student's first night when we show him or her how to coordinate combat footwork with gut-feeling emotional stages. We emphasize the study of natural phenomena as a means to better understand how we operate as human parts of the entirety of all that is.

Perhaps this is the part of our training that is misunderstood and feared by those that I would call morally timid or spiritually immature. Perhaps they think we are worshipping all these different pieces of nature and symbols representing psychological states. Actually, there is no worship at all, only the acknowledgment of the manner in which all pieces operate as interworking parts of the whole. We may occasionally find it helpful to imitate these phenomena of nature, or strive to embody the characteristics of legendary or historical heroic beings. That, however, is a far cry from the accusations that we are involving our students in something unholy or demonic.

Once he or she has gone through that initiation, we go on to encourage the student in the study of tactics and strategy. In other words, the physical realm of awareness. The third portion of the triangle is the exploration of the realm of directed intention, in which we hold in our hearts the firm conviction of that which we work to bring into reality through skillful physical actions and appropriate intellectual tactics.

As far as students being required to investigate these spiritual powers, I can only say that nothing is *required* of anyone in our training halls. However, there is no getting around the fact that the art of ninjutsu is based on these spiritual realizations. Therefore, students negating or ignoring these fundamental teachings could hardly be referred to as practicing the authentic art of ninjutsu.

Q. *Back there in the early 1970s when you first made up your mind to go to Japan in search of ninja training, did you ever imagine that the once-obscure "art of invisibility" would someday be referred to as the major martial art phenomenon of the 1980s?*

A. To be completely frank, I was a bit surprised that it had not been the major martial art of the 1960s and 1970s. All descriptions of the art that I had encountered in the late 60s and early 70s painted it as some sort of ultimate in combat and enlightenment practicality. That is what I had always thought the martial arts were intended to be from the beginning. Ninjutsu seemed to have everything for the warrior—unarmed tactics without limit, practical weapons, use of the environment, healing methods, diet considerations, psychological training, and the unavoidable acknowledgment of those aspects that are best described as being "beyond the mind and body." With all that ninjutsu was reputed to entail, I was amazed to find that no Americans had ever become students of the art in Japan before me. It was shocking to think that no one else before me had thought of going over there to find the art.

But to answer your question, I eventually discovered that they had allowed me to train there because they needed some large training dummies on which to try out the techniques. (Laughing) Of course I did not know that at the time, but my friends at the dojo cheerfully informed me of that fact several years later.

Q. *What form does your personal training take these days? Is there anything* *left for you to learn?*

A. Most definitely. My program now is to visit Japan twice a year for continuing work with Dr. Hatsumi. I have also been traveling to the Himalayan region once a year for training with Tibetan teachers there.

Q. *Is there a Tibetan version of ninjutsu?*

A. No. Ninjutsu is strictly a Japanese phenomenon. It never existed in other countries. However, just as in all Asian countries heavily under the influence of Buddhist teachings, there did evolve a pragmatic protective combat method practiced by certain groups of Tibetan monks. This combat system was handed down through a lineage of Tibetan temple guardians up until the time of the Communist Chinese invasion of Tibet in 1959. These Tibetan teachers I work with in Nepal and India are, of course, not teaching me ninjutsu. However, so many of the roots of the Japanese art reach back across the Himalayas to tantric sources, that what the Tibetans have to offer fits my ninja training perfectly.

Q. *You are away from your dojo more often than you are in it. Does your extensive travel and teaching schedule ever get in the way of your own higher level training?*

A. Interestingly enough, the teaching I do through my seminars and workshops is crucial to my own growth. Teaching is my laboratory. The seminars are my testing grounds. I am constantly faced with new situations, new questions, new challenges, and new people who add to my total collection of experiences. Therefore, my training with new and intermediate students is just as important for my own growth as training with my senior students and even my superiors in Japan.

Q. *Do you feel that there are major differences between the practitioners studying ninjutsu in Japan and the ones studying the art in America?*

A. There are certain cultural aspects of the art that will of course be more recognizable to the Japanese students. We in the West just have to work a little harder to get the true essence of what is being transmitted. But in truth we have more in common with our Japanese counterparts than we have differences.

On both sides of the Pacific, we are still struggling to personalize the arts—to work through all the details and see which parts or aspects are cultural and which are universal. It is one thing to be taught a collection of techniques and become fairly proficient at performing those techniques for others. It is a far different matter to take those example techniques and internalize them to the extent where technique is transcended and the combatant becomes the embodiment of spontaneous art in motion. I find that few persons in the martial arts ever accomplish the attainment of that rare level of total merging with all available levels of power at which we as humans can operate.

Q. *Why do you feel that so few people are able to make it to the level you describe?*

A. I would say that the overwhelming majority of persons in the martial arts, both in Japan and the U.S. as well, lack the personal driving desire to go as far as they possibly can. So many persons become comfortable at lesser levels of skill and stay there the rest of their lives. It is so easy and tempting to be satisfied with mediocrity. But then, it is absolutely no different with anything else in life, is it? For every great architect, there are hundreds of mediocre ones. For every one contributing entrepreneur who is enthralled with his or her work as a producer in society, there are hundreds or maybe thousands of people who are in effect little more than salaried corporate drones. For every one champion in any given sport, there are thousands or maybe millions of people who are in effect self-limiting hackers, just playing around.

There are very few at the top of any area of expertise, when compared with the huge mass of souls who settle for the lower and middle regions of comfortable limited success. Whether we are discussing the martial arts or anything else in life, success is still a matter of commitment. Few persons, it seems, are what could be described as 100-percent committed to going all the way on the warrior path.

Q. *So how about you? Has Shidoshi Stephen Hayes reached that upper level described as being attained by so very few?*

A. I would have to let my life speak for itself. What do you see? Even the grandmaster says the same thing. "Let them watch the way I move. Let them try to outmaneuver or outdo me if they want to. That is how we judge who is or is not qualified to teach the authentic art of ninjutsu."

Rating oneself is a very tricky and dangerous game. It is too easy to allow ourselves to be fooled out of desire or a need for fulfillment. That kind of dishonesty overtakes so many people in the martial arts because there is no reliable and objective system of licensing.

I am sure that every martial artist personally knows of a few characters out there who have gone the route of needing the money, or the attention, or even the self-esteem, so they award themselves the titles like master, tenth-degree, professor, *soke,* etc., even though their actual training, personal experience, and ability to generate results in life are all tragically lacking. The deadly trap of posing as a master is that it then becomes a matter of limiting one's contacts to those of lesser skill and slowly closing off those challenging new areas one is not too comfortable dealing with. And of course that insulation from those things that would provide new knowledge and experience is the first major step toward the death and mummification of a once-living martial artist.

Q. *There seems to be some controversy concerning the meaning, or lack thereof, of belt ranks in ninjutsu. Just how important is ranking in the art of ninjutsu, when it comes to determining what the student's skill level is?*
A. Well, to begin with, my dojo's training method could only be described as a combat-oriented system, so therefore any given license—I do not like the word "rank"—can only indicate the amount of *training experiences* a practitioner has undergone and made his or her own. In all honesty, it would be impossibly difficult to base licensing in a fighting system on results-producing skill. Really, how could we test such a thing?

In a combat system, a belt degree might be compared with a university degree. You go to all the classes, you get all the material, you are tested to some degree on the material you have been shown, and then you head out into the world with your diploma. From that point on, the results you produce are totally up to you. We can show the student all the drills and exercises and strategies and simulated scenarios and then license him or her as having been through it all, but what that student does when confronted by a roaring, murderously intent killer on the street is entirely up to him. We have done the best we could to get the point of the training to the students; now what are they going to do with it?

Q. *How do you handle instructor licensing in your organization? I would imagine that earning a black belt and having the credentials to open up a ninjutsu school with your endorsement in the current market would be something that a lot of people would like to be able to do.*

A. In my own system, it is not possible to be licensed without being highly involved with the people who have gone before to create this art in the Western world. A student has to be actively training with one of our teachers who has taken responsibility for him or her. It is not possible to hold a teaching license without being a part of the greater family. There must be a connection there, an acknowledged feeling of shared friendship. The art is passed on through a highly personalized system of direct transmission, and the belt levels are mere symbols of the student's degree of involvement.

Q. *Can you tell us a little of the background history and current purpose of your Shadows of Iga Society? It really is not at all a martial arts organization in the true sense of the word, is it?*

A. No, not in the sense of an association that gives out rankings and certifies teachers. It is best described as an information exchange network. Ironically, the vast majority of the Shadows of Iga Society members are not practitioners of the art of ninjutsu.

Q. *They are not ninja? Then who are they?*

A. The majority of members are people who want to find out more about the ninja arts before getting involved. A lot of the members are teachers of other martial arts who just want to know more about what is going on in the martial arts world. The information they get from us helps them broaden a little bit what they are teaching in their tae kwon do, kung fu, or jujitsu classes. Some members aren't even martial artists at all. They join for the spiritual insights they might find.

After beginning my training in Japan in 1975, I founded the society as a means of assisting other people just like me who wanted to find out more about this incredible art that was so little known even a decade ago. I chose the name Shadows of Iga as a way to suggest the historical and cultural background of the art, since its roots were in the Iga region of Japan. The society began as an informational organization. The primary benefit of the society has always been to serve as a rallying point for persons who desired more information on how to get involved with the art of ninjutsu. Through our annual Shadows of Iga Festival, the Warrior Quest seminars, and our newsletters, we have been able to assist people in getting involved in the art all over the world.

Q. *What is the current image of the ninja in Japan? Has any progress been made in changing the Japanese public concept of the art?*

A. There is still a long way to go. Old stereotypes die hard, in the Orient as well as in the Western world. To the average Japanese, a ninja is still a sorcerer or wizard, a sly trickster, and not-really-acceptable breaker of rules. I jokingly refer to it as 800 years of bad press. The samurai are the heroes, so where does that leave the ninja? In many ways it resembles the old TV cowboys and Indians prejudice of 1950s America.

Q. *What can be done to alter the Western image of the ninja as an assassin in black?*

A. To be perfectly honest, there are many persons out there who *do not* want to alter the image. Unfortunately, we must acknowledge the new crop of "ninjutsu teachers" who read a few books, saw a magazine or two, and decided that ninjutsu was for them. Since they had no training under an actual master of the art, they believed all the inaccurate stories about assassins and so forth. Perhaps because of certain pathological imbalances in their personalities, they were actually attracted to the dark and creepy image. You can usually tell that a person has had no training in the authentic art of ninjutsu when he emphasizes all the darkness, talks of assassination, and generally radiates sneakiness. That is just flat-out not the true and historical art of ninjutsu as it was handed down by the historical families of Japan. It is a comic book reality, but many people want to believe in it anyway.

Q. *You have amassed quite a bit of notoriety in the past decade—14 books published, BLACK BELT Hall of Fame, seminar tours all over the globe. Are there any negative aspects to that kind of recognition?*

A. Notoriety is a mere by-product. It is nowhere near anything like the goal. Being well-known was not my purpose for journeying to Japan to become an apprentice of the grandmaster of ninjutsu all those years ago. I suppose it could be said, however, that if you do something well, people cannot help but notice. It could also be said that the bigger one's image, the more tempting a target one becomes. It is no secret that there are people out there who growl at the mere printing of my name.

But the good part is that the happy by-products of my work far outshadow the few troubled individuals who choose not to accept me or my message. I suppose that there is no way any one person is going to please everyone, so I concentrate on pleasing myself, bearing in mind of course an awareness of a healthy desire to serve the world as best I can.

It can be so disheartening, all the people out there who desire happiness but have no idea of how to bring it into their lives. They want to be ninja masters but do not want to have to study the art. They are, in effect, their own worst enemies, but cannot see that. I wish there were some way for me to assist them, but they have twisted my image into that of the "bad guy." They see me as some sort of enemy to be pulled down. They would sooner live in agony than be my friend. Crazy, huh?

At least there is a balance. On one hand, I am the target of a few sad little pathetic people who hope to elevate themselves by shooting down my work. On the other hand, all these wonderful friends and opportunities would not have been possible without my decision to seek out the authentic shinobi warrior legacy all those years ago. The hassles pale when compared with the gifts that life has bestowed. That is the art of the ninja in my life. That is what makes it all worth it. That is the message that I have to share from my position at this moment in this powerful legacy that reaches back through Japanese history for almost a millennium.

Q. *That sounds like odd talk coming from a man who made his mark in the world as a teacher of warrior disciplines. It is surprising to hear compassionate words for those whom you see as striking out vengefully at you and your work. That sounds more like a priest than a fighter.*

A. At this point on my path of experience, I would have to say that the ultimately developed shinobi warrior sees life through the eyes of a priest. Even bitter enemies have their lessons to teach us, if only we can be sensitive enough to interpret those lessons from their actions.

Persons interested in further exploring the ninja combat enlightenment methods as taught by Stephen K. Hayes can begin by joining the Shadows of Iga Society. For detailed information, write to the society's correspondence center at:

Shadows of Iga Society
P.O. Box 291947
Kettering, Ohio 45429-0947 USA

NINJA Books from Stephen K. Hayes

Available only from Black Belt Books

NINJA Vol. 1:
Spirit of the Shadow Warrior
by Stephen K. Hayes

Written by the first American *ninjutsu* teacher, this book covers the history of ninjutsu, philosophy, fighting, the mind as a tool of the spirit, active meditation, extended realities and the art of understanding. Fully illustrated techniques with step-by-step photos and instructions. 144 pgs. (ISBN-10: 0-89750-073-3) (ISBN-13: 978-0-89750-073-0)
Book Code 411—Retail $17.95

NINJA Vol. 2:
Warrior Ways of Enlightenment
by Stephen K. Hayes

The first American ever certified to teach *ninjutsu* covers spiritual purity, preparation, methods of rebounding, training for combat and attuning to the universe. Fully illustrated techniques with step-by-step photos and instructions. 160 pgs. (ISBN-10: 0-89750-077-6) (ISBN-13: 978-0-89750-077-7)
Book Code 414—Retail $17.95

NINJA Vol. 3:
Warrior Path of Togakure
by Stephen K. Hayes

Stephen K. Hayes, who has trained personally with *ninjutsu* grandmaster Masaaki Hatsumi in Japan, teaches the warrior quest, enlightened consciousness, ninja invisibility, the body and weapon as one, directing the power of surroundings and contemporary ninja training. Fully illustrated techniques with step-by-step photos and instructions. 144 pgs. (ISBN-10: 0-89750-090-3) (ISBN-13: 978-0-89750-090-6)
Book Code 427—Retail $19.95

NINJA Vol. 5:
Lore of the Shinobi Warrior
by Stephen K. Hayes

The first Westerner responsible for introducing authentic *ninjutsu* to America explores the use of natural body postures and movements, attack angles, striking tools, and dispels popular myths about ninjutsu. Fully illustrated techniques with step-by-step photos and instructions. 160 pgs. (ISBN-10: 0-89750-123-3) (ISBN-13: 978-0-89750-123-1)
Book Code 463—Retail $19.95

NINJA Vol. 6: Secret Scrolls of the Warrior Sage
by Stephen K. Hayes

Legendary *ninjutsu* master Stephen K. Hayes returns to impart four decades of wisdom and insight on his loyal readers. This highly anticipated new book from the best-selling author includes scores of new technique demonstrations, an in-depth discussion of the most effective martial arts mind-set and how to traverse training plateaus in any martial art. Hayes also describes the experiences that made him an internationally recognized warrior and educator, including his bodyguard duties for the Dalai Lama. 228 pgs. (ISBN-10: 0-89750-123-3) (ISBN-13: 978-0-89750-123-1)
Book Code 485—Retail $19.95

NINJA Vol. 4:
Legacy of the Night Warrior
by Stephen K. Hayes

The ancient combat techniques of flowing action, the subtle energy of hands, the fighting methods of the *kunoichi* (the female ninja), the unique sensitivity training to develop fighting intuition—all these are explained by Stephen K. Hayes, the first non-Japanese ever awarded the title of *shidoshi* (teacher of the warrior ways of enlightenment), in his fourth fully illustrated volume for Black Belt Books. 192 pgs. (ISBN-10: 0-89750-102-0) (ISBN-13: 978-0-89750-102-6)
Book Code 437—Retail $19.95